From Within the Clouds

Emmilyne Major

Presentation by *BookLeaf Publishing*

Web: www.bookleafpub.com

E-mail: info@bookleafpub.com

ISBN: 978-93-95784-30-6

First edition 2022

DEDICATION

Dedicated to all of those who I have loved, and
to those I have lost.

Someone

Someone tell me it gets better,
That the loneliness subsides.
That sitting alone on our bathroom floor
Is no way to live our lives.

Someone tell me I've been brave enough,
That I'm stronger than I seem.
Tell me that chasing a goal is safer,
Than going after my dreams.

Someone tell me who to turn to,
When it feels too hard to breathe.
Tell me who to trust, who to love,
What to farewell, and what to grieve.

Someone tell me I am beautiful,
Even though I'll shy away.
Teach me how to talk about pain,
That it's okay to not be okay.

Release

My soul is frozen
Stinging like shards of ice against my mind
Negative thoughts pelt my heart
Like razor blades

Although I have nothing to fear
I don't want to have these thoughts
As if their existence isn't enough
What if they become a reality?

My fingers freeze when I go to type
And yet they manage to wipe away my tears
Because I cry so often
But I seldom tell you the truth

Spell it out for me and I still won't believe it
My heart is too hurt
My soul is too cold
My life is too much

Just breathe they say
But breathing isn't the hard part
Wanting to breathe is the most difficult bit
As instinct no longer reigns in my mind

Ghost

Silently stalking my every move,
Always one step behind me,
Every memory and thought,
Haunting, hurting.

Their hands around my neck,
Each day tightening further,
Unable to forget,
I struggle to let go.

They remember every detail,
Clutching to my regrets and fears,
The fight each day to lose them,
Is a slow, losing one.

Invisible to those around me,
I suffer alone,
Hoping for any respite,
From the demons following me.

Stars

I walk alone down a road made of stars,
Each step illuminating my face,
And every tear I've shed finds it's place,
Within the constellation beneath me.

Agonising thoughts shoot past me,
As a meteor rushing to its destination,
Doing its damage on impact,
Each crater, an aching regret.

A warmth overcomes me,
Fleeting pain, a fear, a memory,
I look up into the sun above,
His heat radiating around me.

Sunlight

I always hated my dark brown eyes.
Pools of inky blackness when seen from afar.
I hated the murky muddy colour,
And envied my blue-eyed siblings.

Until the day came along,
Where the sunlight hit my eyes,
Just at the right angle,
And wild textures burst out of my irises.

I'd never seen this before.
Have they always been so beautiful?
Hints of green and orange amongst the brown.
Peaks and valleys, like a mountain range.

Until the sunlight hides once more,
And my admiration slowly fades away.
Mud fills my irises again,
Now I know what hides in that darkness.

Home

I moved to a town within the clouds,
That normally soar high above me.
I wake up each morning and peer outside,
Finding something I didn't expect to see.

I am greeted with a dense mist,
Hovering silently past my home.
Nothing in this town makes sense,
With ancient architecture no one else admires.

Their city is old, just as the townsfolk are.
Yet even they don't seem to acknowledge
The clouds we live amongst,
And the structures that surround us.

When I stop and look around myself,
At the fog gently hanging over the buildings,
I am looked at like I am outlandish.
Like an outcast.

I have never seen something so haunting,
Yet so beautiful,
As a misty morning atop a mountain,
That I now call my home.

I am living in the clouds,
Unashamedly cherishing
Every second I spend within them,
With no intention of stopping.

Goodnight

And then, just like clockwork,
The negative thoughts come back,
Slowly creeping into my mind
Like low-hanging fog on an eerie winter night.

Silently rolling over my body,
Suffocating me with its painful honesty,
And incessant recounts,
Of every blunder I've ever committed.

The medication helps,
but only for so long.
I spend my days avoiding the pain
And hoping it isn't visible from the outside.

Pause

No one else sees this,
Not like you do.
And it will never be the same,
Not exactly.

They tell you to stop,
And smell the roses.
But I think you should pause
And enjoy more than just flowers.

Sure, look at the roses,
But smell it, watch it sway too,
See the ant crawling up it,
Hear the breeze whooshing past you.

Pause your day,
Witness your world.
Just take that moment,
It could change your life.

You

I've never known a love like this,
At least nothing of this connection.
The pull I feel when we're apart,
Takes me in your direction.

I still vividly remember,
The first day that we met.
I felt the rush within my heart,
My mind was already set.

And every time I see you now,
Those emotions still ignite.
The taste of you upon my lips
I dream about at night.

You've always been a sense of peace,
A stable part of life.
You pick me up when I feel down,
Remind me I'll be alright.

I could never live without you now
I enjoy your company,
A future together would be so nice,
Unless I get hungry.

You won't be around for too much longer,
Although I crave your taste.
You'll always have a spot in my heart
My darling, peanut paste.

Refresh

I feel slightly less alone,
Like the universe has paused it's pain,
Like I'm feeling more like myself,
Like I'm ready to be loved again.

A simple hug, one kind gesture,
A human interaction.
It's refreshing to meet a man,
Who looks beyond first attraction.

A confidence boost for both of us,
Working hard distracts the heart.
I could laugh with you for hours,
Your smile, a work of art.

Wish

I wish the world would give me one more
chance,
A moment of luck, the right stranger's glance.
I wish my stars would align and bring me
something worthwhile,
But waiting around for help was never quite my
style.

I wish I had the strength to wake up with a
smile,
To go about my day-to-day, to go the extra mile.
I wish we'd never met and I'd never felt that
pain,
Being alone is easier than going through that
again.

My hands are open wide, I'm ready to begin,
I wonder if I seem calm from the outside looking
in.
I wish the answer was more simple to receive,
I don't know what's coming next but I choose to
believe.

Spring

The flowers arrived overnight it seems,
Everywhere, they popped up gloriously,
Greeting the gloomy skies above,
With their vibrant colours and scents.

The town, they say, is famous for it,
Tourists come from all around,
To witness this sleepy country town,
Proudly display their beautiful blooms.

Spring has sprung within the clouds,
The bees buzzing busily past my window.
The mood within the town has lifted,
Even the quietest streets are active now.

I am dreading the end of spring,
After the tourists leave and the flowers die.
What's left but the people of this town,
And the memory of a happier time?

Cancel

Can I hit cancel please?
It's getting quite tiresome.
This whole "existing" thing,
I don't think it's for me.

Waking up every day,
Something new to clean,
Cook some food, go to work,
And do it all over again.

If I could cancel my days,
It would bring me so much peace.
No pressure or angst,
Able to enjoy the world around me.

Happiness

Happiness found in hidden places,
In the step of a stranger,
In the colour of a ripe orange.

Found in the scent of pie,
The distant sound of a train,
A pattern in the clouds above me.

I casually search for those moments,
The laughter of a child,
A light turning green as I arrive to it.

Anxiety

On the edge of my seat,
I wait for something to happen,
Anticipating the next move.

Adrenaline floods my veins,
My breaths get shorter,
My heart thumping out of my chest.

I am heating up from within,
My body can't sit still,
Thoughts running wild.

I am alone in my bedroom.
Panic engulfs me relentlessly.
I am tired, when will it end?

Next

The world stares at me
Wondering
Waiting
Anticipating
What will be her next move?
Who will she become?

I step forward
Prepared to greet
Fate
Destiny
What comes next?
Who decides?

My arms open
I am sent a person
A moment
A chance
A feeling, a lesson

I am changed
Impact after impact
I am moulded
Sculpted

Who am I but the result of others?
Learn
Absorb
I continue on

Packing

When I left my childhood home,
I forgot to pack my happiness.
I took all of the joyful memories,
That morphed into homesickness.

I should have packed more hugs,
I need those more often now.
I should have packed my old room,
With the scents and markings within.

One thing I did forget,
That would come in handy now,
Is the courage little me had,
That she left in the walls of her room.

Now I live in someone else's home,
A stranger I pay each week.
There is no love, no passion,
Just blank walls and unfamiliarity.

Footsteps

21

My greatest fear is that someday,
Silence will haunt my every step.
That I may no longer hear the rhythm,
beaten out with each of my footsteps.

Life

A hopeless endeavour,
A hunt for validation,
A craving for happiness,
A longing to be loved.

A painful crusade,
An endless journey,
A want for more,
A life spent wandering.

Carry

If I could carry around,
Your shoulder in my pocket,
And pull it out when I start to cry,
I'd keep it with me always.

If I could carry around,
Your hand in mine,
And squeeze it when I'm afraid,
I'd feel safer every day.

If I could carry around,
Your arms draped over me,
I'd remember the warmth
Of being in your arms.

If I could carry around,
Your smile in my wallet,
I'd have butterflies all day,
I'd smile like when we're together.

If I could carry around,
Your thoughts in my mind,
I'd see how beautiful I am,
And love myself like you do.

Fin

A small statue,
Of a bird and a frog,
Lies comfortably at the end of my bed.

The bird being strangled,
By the frog's hands,
While the bird eats the poor frog's head.

The lesson here,
Is to never give up,
And to never give in to your foes.

Although it is hard,
It's best to push on,
Where you'll end up - who knows!

9 789395 784306